WORLD WAR II

BY LOUIS L. SNYDER

A GROLIER COMPANY

A FIRST BOOK | REVISED EDITION
FRANKLIN WATTS
NEW YORK | LONDON | TORONTO | SYDNEY | 1981

THIS BOOK IS FOR
HARRY, LINDA, BRAD, AND IVAN SNYDER

Cover photograph courtesy of: United Press International

Photos courtesy of: U.S. Navy Photograph: pp. vi, 41, 44, 62 (top); United Press International: pp. 3, 12, 15, 21, 24, 26, 29, 36, 56, 62 (bottom), 64, 69, 72; Institute of Contemporary History and Wiener Library, Limited: p. 8; Freelance Photographers Guild: p. 18; YIVO Institute for Jewish Research: p. 32; Franklin D. Roosevelt Library: pp. 47, 80; U.S. Airforce Photograph; p. 75.

Maps courtesy of Vantage Art, Inc.

Library of Congress Cataloging in Publication Data

Snyder, Louis Leo, 1907–
    World War II.

    (A First book)
    Rev. ed. of: The first book of World War II.
    Includes index.
    Summary: Spotlights the important events and people of World War II.
    1. World War, 1939–1945—Juvenile literature. [1. World War, 1939–1945.] I. Title.
D743.7.S5   1981   940.53   81–5021
ISBN 0–531–04333–9   AACR2

CONTENTS

WORLD WAR II

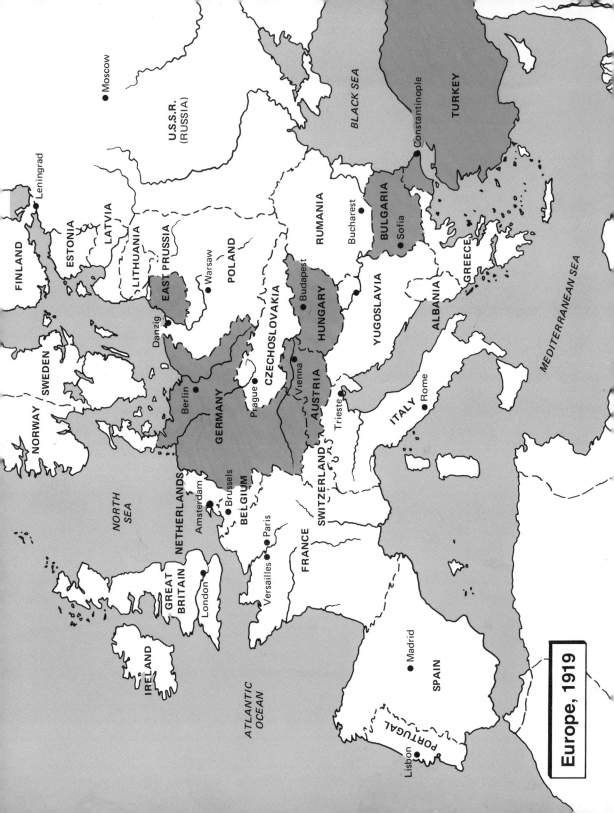

Europe, 1919

INTRODUCTION

It was the most widespread and costly war in the history of
mankind.

It lasted for six years of conquest, slaughter, misery, famine,
and death.

It was fought by more people—about 70 million in all—with
more machines and weapons, over a greater area than
any war in history.

The cost in human lives was tremendous and loss of property
was so great that we can set no proper figure on either.

All this to rid the world of Germany's Hitler, Italy's Mussolini,
and Japan's Tojo.

*Opposite: this is the map of
Europe after World War I;
by 1941 Hitler would control
most of it (see page 35).*

BLITZKRIEG—
LIGHTNING WAR

September 1, 1939. Remember it well—it was one of the most important dates in all history. The mighty German Army, led by dictator Adolf Hitler, crashed across the borders of Poland.

First came *Stuka* dive bombers, with shrieking whistles in their wings to strike fear into the hearts of the Polish people. German aircraft blasted Polish planes on the ground. Then they bombed railroads and highways and dropped their deadly cargoes to smash Warsaw and other cities. It was a violent surprise attack by massed air forces.

Next came soldiers on motorcycles and crews of armored cars and tanks to prepare the way. Finally, regular infantry—the foot soldiers—trained to the minute, moved in to finish the job.

This was a new kind of war. Germans called it *Blitzkrieg,* which means "lightning war." They had the most powerful force in the world with which to wage it. They were lucky to have good weather. The ground was level and just right for this kind of speedy attack.

Now the Russians, who had signed a pact with the Germans, pushed into Poland from the east. Russians and Germans were going to divide the country between them.

Poland had no chance whatever against these two great powers. Her little army had to fight on two fronts. Within two weeks Warsaw was in German hands. In a little over a month the Germans had control of the countryside as Russians moved in from the east.

This was the way World War II began.

Incendiary bombs rain down on Warsaw.

ROAD TO WAR

The causes of war are never simple and that is true of World War II. There were many causes. Several arose out of World War I.

Four empires were swept away in 1918 after World War I —German, Austro-Hungarian, Turkish, and Russian. The Germans were bitter about the Treaty of Versailles at the end of the war. They lost all their colonies and about one-eighth of their land in Europe. They had to return Alsace-Lorraine to France. Their proud navy, second only to that of Britain, was swept from the seas. Their army was cut down to 100,000 men.

Germans were angry about Poland, their neighbor to the east. After World War I, Poland was given an outlet to the sea. This strip of territory was called the Polish Corridor. It ran right through German lands. The Germans never forgave the Allies of World War I for splitting their country into two parts.

The Allies hoped that World War I would be "the war to end all wars"—but it did not turn out that way. Sad to say, that war, instead of healing wounds, actually created new ones. When Germany grew strong again, she tried to take revenge.

During World War I the countries allied against Germany borrowed billions of dollars from the United States, promising to pay it back over a period of sixty-two years. They expected to get the money from Germany by demanding reparations, or payments, for war damage. But Germany had no way to pay so much money.

Starting in 1929 there came a worldwide depression, a time when millions of people were poor and out of work. The Depression hit Germany hard. She had lost almost everything

4

she had in the war and she was in debt to the victor nations.

In such times, when people are cold and hungry and see no hope ahead, it is sometimes easy for one determined person to drive them where he wants them to go. Such people may become dictators. They dictate to the people; they tell them exactly what to do. They promise everything if only they—the dictators—are allowed to run the country. Dictators believe that human beings are like animals—strong tigers and weak lambs. They think of themselves as tigers, and believe they should rule the lambs.

After World War I three strong dictators arose. They were Hitler in Germany, Mussolini in Italy, and Tojo in Japan. These men said that democracy was "a corpse." In a free country they might have found it hard to make the people follow them, however fine their promises. But Germans, Italians, and Japanese had never known real freedom. Most were used to following strong leaders instead of working out their own problems in a representative government.

Benito Mussolini became dictator of Italy in 1922. He was a journalist who had written a number of revolutionary pamphlets. His followers were called Fascists. They believed in a dictatorial government that would suppress opposition by force. When he first came into power, Mussolini won the loyalty of the people by making improvements at home. He built new roads, new houses, new factories. One of his proud boasts was that he had made the Italian trains run on time! But he demanded that the people obey him absolutely. Like other dictators, he held control of the army and the police. Anyone who refused to obey was sent to prison or even killed.

Mussolini's real ambition was to rule a great colonial empire. He said that Italy had too little land and too many people. He felt Italy needed more land in which to grow and become

5

a great nation. He wanted the whole Mediterranean Sea to become an Italian lake—*mare nostrum,* which means "our sea." Mussolini glorified war and sent his armies into Africa to take new land by force.

General Hideki Tojo was the leader of the war party in Japan. He won power in that tiny island by promising the people an empire in Asia. Under Tojo's leadership Japan attacked China in 1931. In 1932 Japan seized the rich province of Manchuria and renamed it Manchukuo.

THE MAN CALLED ADOLF HITLER

The third, and most important, of this trio of twentieth-century dictators was Adolf Hitler. Americans thought he was a comical figure with his Charlie Chaplin mustache and staring eyes. But there was nothing funny about this squat little man with his raucous voice and jabbing fingers.

He was not even a German. He was an Austrian who came to Germany and built up a political party called National Socialists, or Nazis. He was a gifted orator who had the power to arouse huge groups of people and turn them against others. Germans suffering from hurt pride after the loss of World War I turned eagerly to him. This strange man promised the jobless and angry Germans that he would win back their lost lands and make them a great nation again.

Only a few Germans understood the real character of this man—his seething hatred for Jews, Poles, and Gypsies, his brutality, his lack of decency. He was probably not insane but he was highly neurotic. Some Germans secretly called him the *Teppichfresser* ("carpet eater"), because, they said, when he was crossed he would fall to the floor in rage and chew the carpet!

This man, with his promises of German glory, became chancellor in 1933. He began to arm the country to get what he called *Lebensraum,* or "living space." He meant to take land from other nations. He knew that the only way he could get that was through war—and he was willing to risk it.

It is always difficult for historians to blame any one person for starting a war. But most historians agree that Hitler helped to push the German people into a war they did not want.

HITLER LEADS THE GERMANS

Under Hitler's government (called the Third Reich), the Germans began to hope again. But he took away their freedom and the democracy they had set up after World War I. He was a harsh dictator. To go against his wishes was to risk death. He was the leader—the *Führer*—and his word was law.

Hitler was driven by the idea that the Germans were a special "race." But there is no such thing as a "German race" any more than there is an "American race." Hitler thought the "German race" was greater than all others. He felt it should rule everywhere. A favorite Nazi slogan was: "Today, Europe. Tomorrow, the world!"

In World War I Hitler had been a dispatch-bearer and he loved the idea of war. "For the good of the German people," he said, "we must wish for a war every fifteen or twenty years. An army whose sole purpose it is to preserve peace ends up playing at soldiers."

This man would lead Germany to tragedy.

Once he had gained full power, Hitler began to round up, imprison, and kill German Jews. He told the German people that Germany's downfall in World War I was largely the fault of Jews. His Nazi followers believed him. In the course of the war Hitler slaughtered more than 6 million Jews and millions of Poles and Gypsies.

Another evil thing Hitler did was to burn books that spoke for the freedom and dignity of the human spirit. He knew that people would be easier to lead once they got it out of their heads that they could or should rule themselves.

Hitler's deeds of violence, especially his attempt to destroy all Jews in Germany, horrified people everywhere. He shook the whole world as it had not been shaken since the days of other cruel dictators—Caligula of ancient Rome and Ivan the Terrible of Russia.

This was the man who led Germany into a massive war. The blame for starting World War II rests mostly on Adolf Hitler.

THE AXIS CHOOSES WAR

The Axis leaders—Hitler, Mussolini, and Tojo—felt strong and sure of themselves. It was impossible to reason with them. They wanted war. The Allies—Britain, France, and later the Soviet Union and the United States—united to stop them.

Adolf Hitler: "Today, Europe.
Tomorrow, the world!"

As early as 1936, Nazi Germany and Fascist Italy joined together in what was known as the Rome-Berlin Axis. It was called "Axis" because all European states were supposed to revolve around these two great powers—just as a wheel turns on its axis.

Japan joined the Axis in 1940 because it had the same ideas of aggression. This agreement was called the Pact of Steel. The three Axis powers wanted more land, more power.

Both Hitler and Mussolini wanted more space for their people, either in Europe or in North Africa. Tojo and the Japanese militarists wanted to carve out a huge empire in the Far East.

The only way to reach their goals was to go to war.

STEPS OF AGGRESSION

As early as 1938 Hitler began his moves of aggression. On March 12, 1938, he sent his troops into nearby Austria. No one lifted a hand to stop him when he took Austria and made it a part of Germany.

Next Hitler looked to Czechoslovakia. This new democratic republic had been formed out of a part of the old Austro-Hungarian Empire after World War I. It included the region called the Sudetenland. There were many Germans living in this area. Hitler falsely claimed that they were mistreated. He threatened to seize the Sudetenland by force.

Both France and Russia had signed treaties to defend Czechoslovakia. If Hitler attacked, they had promised to come to her help. If war came, Britain would surely be drawn into it. And Britain was not prepared for war.

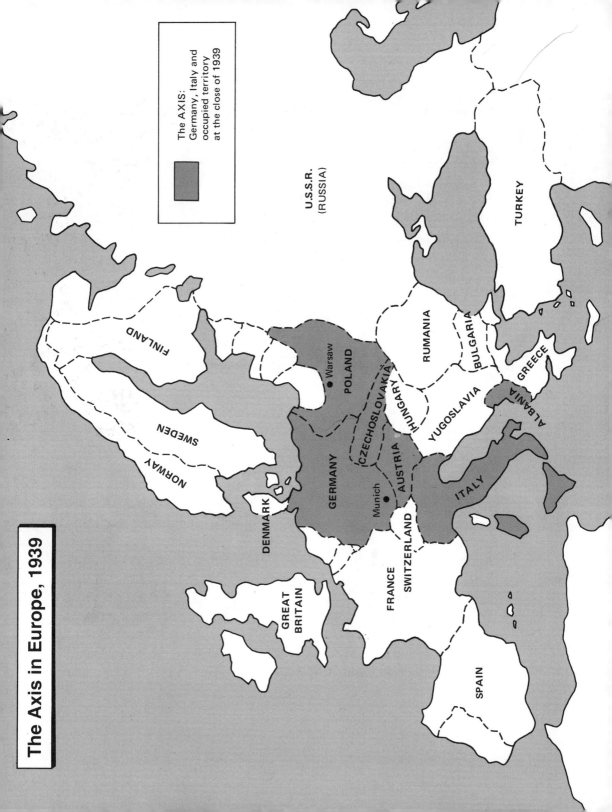

The Axis in Europe, 1939

The AXIS: Germany, Italy and occupied territory at the close of 1939

GREAT BRITAIN

NORWAY

SWEDEN

FINLAND

DENMARK

U.S.S.R. (RUSSIA)

GERMANY

POLAND

● Warsaw

● Munich

CZECHOSLOVAKIA

AUSTRIA

HUNGARY

RUMANIA

YUGOSLAVIA

BULGARIA

ALBANIA

GREECE

TURKEY

ITALY

SWITZERLAND

FRANCE

SPAIN

Survivors of torpedoed ship
Athenia

In an effort to keep the peace, Britain's elderly Prime Minister, Neville Chamberlain, and the French Premier, Édouard Daladier, went to Germany to talk to Hitler. They met both Hitler and Mussolini at the city of Munich. There, on September 29, 1938, all four signed the document known as the Munich Pact.

By the Munich Pact war was stopped at the last minute. But it was done at a cruel price, and on Hitler's own terms. The document gave Germany 10,000 square miles (25,899 sq km) of Czech territory with more than 3 million people. The broken little country was left at the mercy of the Nazis.

Chamberlain returned to London waving a piece of paper. He assured the British people that he had brought "peace in our time."

Seldom has a statesman been more mistaken. And no one asked the Czechs how they felt about it. They were betrayed and there would be no peace for them.

Before the year was over, both the British and French had reason to suspect that Hitler had his eyes on Poland.

The French had a treaty with Poland protecting her from invasion. The British, too, announced that they would fight to preserve Poland's independence. On September 1, 1939, Hitler invaded Poland. Always sure of himself, he thought that both the French and British were bluffing.

They were not. On September 3, Britain and France declared war on Germany.

SINKING OF THE *ATHENIA*

In World War I the Germans had enraged the American people when one of their U-boats sank the passenger steamer

Lusitania. That was one among many events which brought the United States into that war.

World War II was only nine hours old on a beautiful September day in 1939. Passengers on board the *Athenia,* a 13,500-ton passenger ship of the Donaldson Atlantic Line, voyaging from Liverpool to Montreal, were enjoying themselves at sea.

Suddenly someone cried: "Look! There's a torpedo!"

Almost at once there was a crashing explosion. The unarmed ship began to sink. Women and children rushed into lifeboats.

There were 1,417 people aboard that unlucky ship. One hundred twelve lives were lost, of whom 69 were women and 16 children.

Both British and Americans were appalled by the disaster. Nazi propaganda blamed it on the British, saying Churchill had ordered the ship sunk to set up a new *Lusitania* case.

That was nonsense and few people believed it. Instead, the sinking warned the world that Hitler would do anything to break British control of the seas.

THE SIT-DOWN WAR

There was a strange interlude in the West for a short time after the war began. People began to call it "the phony war." The Germans named it the *Sitzkrieg,* which means "sit-down war."

The French dug in behind their great Maginot Line—a long series of underground forts running along the border between France and Germany. The Germans stayed behind

Civilians at an entrance to the Maginot Line

their Siegfried Line, or West Wall, which they had built above ground. It was much weaker than the Maginot Line.

Both Allied and German troops could see each other. One of the reasons for this lack of action was the fact that the winter of 1939–40 was one of the worst in memory. Another reason was that Hitler believed he could come to terms with the Allies. Then he would turn against the Russians and say to the Allies: "See, we Germans don't like the Russian Communists any more than you do. Look how strong we are. Join us in our crusade against the Bolsheviks!"

That "sit-down war" in the West would not last long.

LIGHTNING WAR IN THE WEST

By this time the Allies refused to be taken in any longer by Hitler's lies. They paid no attention to his peace offering.

Suddenly, in early April, 1940, Hitler attacked Denmark and Norway. Denmark was taken in a single day. Norway held out only until June. Hitler's *Blitzkrieg* was like a knife cutting through butter.

A month later Hitler struck again. He invaded Holland and Belgium. German tanks, followed by infantry, crashed across the borders of these two small countries. Parachutists took airfields, bridges, and railroads. The German Air Force, or *Luftwaffe,* bombed the center of Rotterdam, in Holland, leaving it in flames.

At this time Winston Churchill became prime minister of England. The British people hoped he would find a quick way out of the war. "I have nothing to offer but blood, toil, tears, and sweat," he said.

RETREAT: MIRACLE
AT DUNKERQUE

May 1940. Those were dark days for the Allies. They had fought hard but they could not halt the Nazi advance into Belgium.

The northeastern corner of France was in danger. It was guarded by French troops and by a British Expeditionary Force (BEF). Their task was to keep the Germans from Paris.

The small Belgian army could not stop the Germans. King Leopold was about to surrender. This would be a serious blow to the Allies. Belgians were guarding one flank, or side, of the Allied front.

Hitler saw his chance. He sent a *Panzer* (tank) column racing westward to the English Channel. The idea was to cut off French and British troops and catch them in a trap.

The Allies pulled back to Dunkerque on the coast of France. It was the only port not in German hands. Allied troops there had to leave the European mainland or be captured.

What to do? Between the retreating Allied troops and the Germans there were several floodgates used to protect Dunkerque from the waters of the North Sea. The British opened the floodgates so that the water would flow in and hold up the Germans.

It was a smart move, but actually it did not slow up the Germans enough. They kept moving on. Meanwhile, their aircraft struck at the Allied armies.

Nearly a half million British and French, with a few Dutch troops, poured into the small city of Dunkerque. They were forced into smaller and smaller space. They moved to the

Rescue at Dunkerque

beaches—with only the sea in front of them. Would they make it?

For a few days Allied planes managed to control the air. They were helped by cloudy weather, which hid them from German antiaircraft guns. The rear guard fought desperately on the outskirts of Dunkerque. But the men crowding onto the beaches knew that time was running out. Many of them were wounded, sick, or dying. It seemed they would all be butchered by the Germans.

Then came Operation Dynamo. A strange rescue fleet set out from England. Never before did such a fleet go to war! There were motorboats, lifeboats, fishing boats, navy whalers, tugboats, sailboats, Channel ferries, sloops, minesweepers— almost anything that would float.

These boats were manned by every kind of Englishman. There were bankers and dentists, taxicab drivers and clerks, fishermen and policemen. There were old men whose skins looked fiery red against their white hair. There were bright-faced young Sea Scouts, off on a grim heroic adventure. They were all wet, chilled, weary, and hungry. They were unarmed, but they sailed bravely toward Dunkerque into waters covered with the oil of sunken ships.

Some skippers steered by the flames from Dunkerque. Others just followed in line. Some lost their lives in the darkness when warships cut their little crafts into two. Others were battered and broken by German fighter planes. Still the strange fleet sailed on while the British planes dropped bombs to put a wall of fire between the retreating forces and the Germans who were chasing them.

As the boats approached the beaches, men waded out by the thousands to board them. Others dropped from the ruined piers. Packed beyond the limits of safety, the boats sailed back to England only to return for more men.

19

Out of the rescue boats onto the soil of England stepped an army of dirty, sleepy, hungry men. They were so tired they could hardly walk. One reporter said that they brought with them half the dog population of Belgium and France.

"Some of the dogs were shell-shocked. They whimpered but the men didn't!"

Dunkerque was a turning point in World War II. What seemed to be a great defeat was turned into a great moral victory—the defeated soldiers performed so splendidly that they lived to fight another day. Carried out under the eyes and fire of the enemy, the retreat saved a British army.

The retreat also inspired the greatest voice in England. After the miracle of Dunkerque, Churchill made this proud challenge:

"We shall fight on the seas and oceans. We shall fight with growing confidence and growing strength in the air. We shall defend our island, whatever the cost may be. We shall fight on the beaches. We shall fight on the landing grounds. We shall fight in the fields and in the streets. We shall fight in the hills. We shall never surrender!"

BRITAIN FINDS HER WAR LEADER: WINSTON CHURCHILL

He was fearless, energetic, gifted with a driving zeal. Short, stocky, with a round face and sparkling eyes, he always waved a giant cigar.

Winston Churchill

His name was Winston Spencer Churchill, son of Lord Randolph Churchill and an American mother, Jenny Jerome. He had taken a prominent part in World War I. To his political enemies he was a troublemaker. In the days just before the war, London was covered with huge signs bearing the words: "What price Churchill?" He had long warned about the dangers facing Europe from Hitler.

Churchill was the popular symbol of British determination. On May 11, 1940, he became prime minister at a time that was critical for Britain. "I was sure I would not fail," he said. "I slept soundly and had no need for cheering dreams."

The man with the cigar gave Britons the leadership for which they had waited. He was a magnificent orator and his golden words gave spirit and drive to his fellow countrymen.

"You ask, what is our policy? I will say: it is to wage war, by sea and air, with all our might and with all the strength that God gave us: to wage war against a monstrous tyranny, never surpassed in the dark, lamentable catalog of human crime."

This great man showed his country the way to victory: rejection of all thought of surrender; action against Hitler and his allies at every opportunity; friendship with the United States; and alliance with any country willing to fight the Nazis.

Churchill's contributions to victory defy summary. In a moment of great peril, this man of cherubic face and iron heart brought fresh energy to the British people.

MECHANIZED SHARKS OF THE SEA

From the beginning there were battles on the Atlantic Ocean. Because the British navy was very strong on the surface of the seas, the Germans used a great fleet of submarines. They were called U-boats (undersea boats).

In World War I, from 1914 to 1918, the Germans had sent out their U-boats on single missions. Now they hunted in "wolf packs," with a fleet of supply ships for refueling and making minor repairs at sea. During the night the U-boats would travel at full speed on the surface. Throughout the day they would go under and wait for Allied ships to pass. Churchill said: "The only thing that ever really frightened me during the war was the U-boat peril."

It was called the Battle of the Atlantic. It was a deadly game of hide-and-seek played over endless miles of ocean.

To meet this threat, Allied ships moved in convoys guarded by small warships called destroyers. From these sleek, fast destroyers huge "ash cans," filled with explosives, were thrown overboard to smash the submarines.

The battle moved to and fro across the whole of the Atlantic. As soon as the German U-boats found it too hot in one area, they went somewhere else.

Germany's U-boats took a terrible toll of Allied shipping. The Allies had to meet this challenge if the war was to be won. Later we shall see how they handled the U-boat threat.

FALL OF FRANCE

With the British driven back to their island, the Germans overran the continent of Europe.

The French believed that theirs was the finest army in the world. They felt safe behind their Maginot Line. But Hitler went right around the line. The huge French armies reeled

*The face of defeat: a Frenchman
reacts to German occupation.*

back in retreat. Before long the Germans were hammering at the gates of Paris.

The roads were jammed with people trying to escape. They pushed wagons, baby carriages, anything that would move. Then the Nazi planes came swooping out of the sky and poured death and destruction on these helpless people.

Within a few weeks all of northern France was occupied by Nazi hordes. Mussolini, knowing that France was about to fall, declared war on France and Britain.

On June 17, 1940, a German officer hurried to a garden behind the front lines where Hitler was pacing nervously.

"My Leader," said the officer, "the French have given up. Marshal Pétain has just spoken on the radio. He said, 'The continuation of the struggle against an enemy superior in numbers is futile. It is with a heavy heart I say we must cease the fight.'"

Then a curious thing happened. Adolf Hitler was so pleased with his victory that he could not control his legs. His knees jerked up and down as if he were doing a jig of joy.

The formal surrender was signed on June 22, 1940, in a little clearing in the forest of Compiègne. That was exactly where Germany had given up to the French at the end of World War I. It was a sad day for the French—and the Allies.

THE BRITISH FIGHT BACK: THE BATTLE OF BRITAIN

Now Britain stood alone, and the German troops sang,
"We challenge the lion of England,
For the last and decisive cup,
We judge and we say

Hitler's joy on fall of France

An Empire breaks up.
Listen to the engine singing—onward to the foe!
Listen, in your ears it's ringing—onward to the foe!
BOMBS, OH BOMBS, OH BOMBS ON ENGLAND!"

Hundreds of German *Stuka* dive-bombers, *Dorniers,* and *Heinkels* roared over the English Channel and dropped their cargoes of death. They came mostly at night. They were trying to soften up England for a German invasion. It was to be called Operation Sea Lion.

"This wicked man Hitler," said Churchill, "has now resolved to break down our famous island race."

London was heavily hit. Bombs fell everywhere—on the slums and on Buckingham Palace. Londoners will never forget the night the German bombs started 1,500 separate fires in the heart of the city. Old and famous buildings were wrecked.

Adolf Hitler just did not know the courage and strength of the people he was trying to beat down. The British people remained firm and calm while night after sleepless night the bombs fell on their cities. There was no panic. From king to clerk to office boy they showed an astonishing spirit. The two young princesses, Elizabeth and Margaret Rose, stayed in England during the heavy air attacks.

The British worked out ways to defend against the air raids. By radar, an electronic beam that bounces off objects in space, they could detect enemy planes far away. "Spotters" watched the skies night and day. Antiaircraft guns ringed the cities. The British even hung piano wire from balloons, and some Nazi planes were caught in it. Thousands of men, women, and children acted as fire watchers.

But most important of all was the Royal Air Force—the RAF. It was made up of just a few hundred young fighter pilots. Some were not yet twenty years old. In speedy *Hurricanes* and *Spitfires* they rose to challenge the Germans.

In three months these young pilots destroyed well over 1,000 Nazi planes. The Germans were forced to give up their plan for invading Britain.

The Battle of Britain was the first air war in history. It was also the first German defeat of World War II. The British people knew what they owed to the tireless young pilots of the RAF. In a speech before the House of Commons, Winston Churchill said, "Never in the field of human conflict was so much owed by so many to so few."

TRAITORS HELP THE NAZIS

In smashing his way to control of all Europe, Hitler had the help of leaders who betrayed their own countries. They were known as "collaborators." They did all they could to help Hitler and his invading armies. They believed that Germany would win—and they wanted to be on the winning side.

One of the most infamous was Vidkun Quisling of Norway. His name, "Quisling," came to mean any person who deserted his own country and went over to the enemy.

Quisling ruled Norway for five years in the full glory of Hitler's approval. When the Nazi government crumbled in his country, he was shot by a Norwegian firing squad.

In France, General Henri Pétain, who had been a hero in World War I, gave his help to the Germans. So did Pierre Laval. Pétain was later sentenced to life imprisonment. The swarthy, beetle-browed Laval, whose name was cursed by the furious French public, was executed by firing squad. His last words were: *"Vive la France!"* ("Long live France!").

28

*A rocket bomb results in
devastation of homes in part of London.*

THE NAZI DICTATOR AS MASTER OF EUROPE

Who could believe it? By the spring of 1941 the loud little man with the Charlie Chaplin mustache was the master of all Europe!

Hitler seemed to be unbeatable. He had changed Germany's size from 180,976 to 323,360 square miles (468,726 to 837,499 sq km), and had set up a new German empire. Germany's population jumped from about 65 million to some 106 million.

To control all Europe Hitler had 40,000 airplanes, 180 U-boats, 363,171 tons of surface navy, 214 infantry divisions, and 12 *Panzer* (tank) divisions.

Against the Nazi dictator was pitted the power of the British Commonwealth of Nations. Added to that was a world opinion opposed to Nazi indecency and Nazi aggression.

There was also something Hitler had not counted on— the resources and power of the United States. Americans had watched with increasing dismay as the Nazi war machine trampled on one European country after another. Americans did not like the idea of having to live in a world controlled from Nazi Berlin.

REVOLT AGAINST THE NAZI "NEW ORDER"

The people of Europe were not happy about being forced into Hitler's "New Order."

There were Poles, Czechs, Danes, Norwegians, Dutch, Belgians, French, Yugoslavs, and Greeks. Many were forced to work in factories producing arms for the Nazi war machine. It was plain slave labor.

The peoples of Europe refused to stay beaten. Many of them carried on war behind the lines—against their German conquerors. The Nazi dictator never understood that people would not willingly remain slaves. They were ready to die in the struggle for their freedom.

Czechs wrecked trucks and blew up ammunition dumps. In the factories they put powdered glass into oil and poured sugar into gasoline to ruin it. At their machines they carefully made bullets and shells which would not explode—anything to harm the enemy.

The Dutch killed Nazi officers and soldiers. In the middle of the night they would put weights on the bodies and then throw them into the canals, where they would not be found.

The French resisted Hitler by blowing up bridges and derailing trains. They published patriotic newspapers right under the noses of the enemy.

Everywhere throughout Europe there were brave people who helped Allied prisoners to escape.

The peoples of Europe became united in their hatred for the invaders.

German occupation forces reacted violently. When one of their men was killed, they took hostages, or prisoners. They would arrest anybody in sight, including children, and put them to death in revenge. They warned, "Fifty Frenchmen for every German killed."

Hundreds of innocent men, women, and children died.

One of Hitler's most brutal lieutenants was Reinhard Heydrich, "the Savage Hangman." Czech patriots killed him,

*Polish Jews were marched off
by Hitler's Nazi guards.*

and the Nazis took terrible revenge. In the little Czecho-slovakian village of Lidice, the Nazis lined up every man, 190 in all, on a grassy meadow and machine-gunned them. The 195 women in town were sent to a concentration camp. And the 82 children were scattered abroad. Then every trace of Lidice was destroyed, even its graveyard, and the ground was plowed flat.

"The name Lidice has been wiped from the face of the earth forever!" shouted the Nazi radio.

But the Nazi radio was wrong. Today, at the spot where the little village stood, thousands of visitors pass by to see the monument that has made Lidice immortal.

The policy of terror did not work—and the world does not forget.

UNITED STATES: ARSENAL OF DEMOCRACY

Americans had hoped to stay out of the war. But as the struggle went on they began to see that they might have to join the fight in some way.

The growing power of Hitler threatened the rights not only of Europeans but also of Americans. The United States was the only country which could outmatch and even outstrip the industrial might of Hitler's Europe. Without her help the British could not have gone on after the fall of France.

By this time the British were in a bad way. They had spent most of their money buying food and weapons from the United States. They could no longer pay for desperately needed supplies. President Roosevelt and the U.S. Congress now agreed to lend Britain the supplies she needed.

In early March, 1941, the U.S. Congress passed the Lend-Lease Bill. It was to help "any country whose defense the President deemed vital for the United States." Britain could now receive goods from the United States by sale, exchange, or loan. Churchill called this "the most unsordid act in the history of any nation."

The Lend-Lease program was vital in saving Britain from Hitler.

In August, 1941, President Franklin D. Roosevelt and Prime Minister Winston Churchill met off the coast of New-foundland to draw up a statement of war aims. It was called the Atlantic Charter. It pledged allegiance to democracy and promised to work for a world in which all nations would be equal "after the destruction of the Nazi tyranny."

In Roosevelt's words, America now became "the arsenal of democracy." From her farms poured the food, from her factories the weapons that would finally mean the end of the dictators.

NAZI GERMANY TURNS ON THE SOVIET UNION

A great turning point in the war came when Hitler decided to break with Stalin. Suddenly, on Sunday morning, June 22, 1941, Germany turned on her former ally. On this same day, back in 1812, the French conqueror Napoleon Bonaparte had attacked Russia. Hitler, who fancied himself a second Napoleon, made the same mistake.

Hitler's Europe, 1941

The AXIS and occupied territory

The greatest extent of Hitler's invasion of Russia

U.S.S.R. (RUSSIA)

Stalingrad

Yalta

Moscow

Leningrad

TURKEY

FINLAND

SWEDEN

NORWAY

POLAND

RUMANIA

Ploieşti

BULGARIA

CZECHOSLOVAKIA

HUNGARY

GREECE

Lidice

AUSTRIA

YUGOSLAVIA

ALBANIA

GERMANY

ITALY

DENMARK

Rotterdam

BELGIUM

Compiègne

SWITZERLAND

Paris

FRANCE

Dunkirk

Calais

GREAT BRITAIN

London

SPAIN

PORTUGAL

*Civilian homes were bombed to rubble
in the battle for Stalingrad.*

Three huge German armies crossed the Russian border without meeting any great resistance. They headed for Leningrad in the north, Moscow in the center, and Stalingrad in the south.

"Russia is broken!" shouted Hitler. "She will never rise again!"

At first many of the Russian people welcomed Hitler because they thought he had come to free them from their own dictator, Joseph Stalin. But Hitler proved to be even worse, they felt, than Stalin. He put many Russians to death and treated the rest as slaves. The Russian people rose to defend their homeland.

The Russians astonished the whole world by their fierce resistance. The soldiers fought hard, but so did old men, women, and children. They even burned their own homes and factories. They blew up bridges. They dynamited their huge dams. They destroyed everything in the path of the Germans.

When they were surrounded, the Russians fought even harder. Like early American Indians, they disappeared into the forests, coming out only at night to smash the railroads or kill the German guards.

Help came at last from Britain and America in the form of war matériel.

Hitler was so sure of his own strength that he believed Russia would fall in six weeks. He was wrong. He did not reckon with the severe Russian winter. His soldiers did not even have winter clothing. And the Russian winter of 1941 turned out to be the worst anyone could remember.

Caught in the icy mud, the huge German war machine slowed down to a crawl on the Russian plains. Hitler, who boasted that he never was wrong, had to explain to his people. He said, "We made a mistake about one thing. We did not know how strong the Russians were."

On August 19, 1942, the Germans began their first direct attack on Stalingrad. For three months a savage battle raged for this Russian city. So closely were the opposing forces matched that the capture of one short street, or even one building, was big news. Shells churned the rubble day after day. A huge German army outside the city struck again and again. But Stalingrad held out.

Soon the Germans were in full flight along a front of many hundreds of miles. The retreat was just like that of Napoleon's army in 1812. The plains of Russia were filled with smashed and burned war machines, wrecked vehicles, and the twisted figures of the dead.

The siege of Stalingrad was a disaster for Adolf Hitler.

It was clear by now that the years of easy victory were over for the Nazi *Führer*. His armies were on the defensive on three fronts. General Rommel, his "Desert Fox," had been beaten in North Africa. The Russians halted his troops in the Russian steppes. There was certain to be an Allied invasion in the West.

A world coalition had risen in anger against the screeching little man and his fanatical followers. The time for boasting was past.

PEARL HARBOR: JAPAN ATTACKS

In the autumn of 1941, while the war in Europe was going on in fury, there came dangerous signals from the Far East.

Relations between Washington and Tokyo were becoming steadily worse. Japanese sea and air power was growing in the Far East and their warlords were calling for action. For the United States this was bad news. If the Japanese became masters of the Pacific, they would interfere with American trade there. It was clear that Japan, like Nazi Germany and Fascist Italy, was bent on a program of conquest.

The Japanese resented what they called American interference in their plans for an empire in the Pacific area. They felt that Washington stood in the way to further conquests. For the time being they did not dare to make an open break. But they were encouraged by Hitler's early successes in Europe. They, too, like Hitler and Mussolini, wanted to seize more "living space."

At 7:55 on the morning of December 7, 1941, a messenger boy pedaled his bicycle toward the American naval station at Pearl Harbor, in Hawaii. He carried a telegram from General George C. Marshall, the Chief of Staff in Washington, to the commanding officer at Pearl Harbor. The note warned the naval station to be on the alert for a Japanese attack.

Suddenly there was a tremendous explosion.

"Wow!" said the messenger boy. "That's not a joke!"

He dived into a ditch. He had to stay there for the next several hours while bombs fell all around him.

There had been signs earlier that something was wrong. At 6:45 that morning an American destroyer, the *Ward,* had found and sunk a Japanese midget submarine in waters where no Japanese warships were allowed to be. Two army privates, working at a radar station, spotted planes many miles away. They were worried, but their lieutenant said that the planes were probably American B-17's.

It was Sunday morning and most of the ship and plane crews were on holiday leave.

Then it happened. Flying low out of the morning haze came the first wave of Japanese bombers. The round red emblem of Japan shone on their wings. The bombs began to drop.

39

It was a murderous attack. The battleship *Arizona* was almost completely destroyed by a direct hit. The *Oklahoma,* struck by many torpedoes, turned over and sank in shallow water. In all, some fourteen big warships and many smaller ships were wrecked or damaged. United States planes were smashed to bits on the ground before they had a chance to rise. In a matter of minutes American naval and air power in the Hawaiian Islands was paralyzed. Nearly 2,500 soldiers, sailors, and civilians died in the blazing inferno.

In Washington, Secretary of State Cordell Hull got news of the disaster quickly. Before he recovered from the shock, an aide came into his office and told him that two Japanese envoys were waiting outside to see him.

"What do they want?" Mr. Hull asked.

"They have a note for you, sir."

"While bombs are falling on Pearl Harbor! Tell them to wait."

Mr. Hull let the two Japanese remain a while in the outer office before calling them in. He read the note, which he found insulting. Then he let the envoys have it!

Mr. Hull had been born and raised in the hills of Tennessee. He knew some vivid curse words, and he is said to have used them freely on the Japanese envoys. Usually a man in his position would not speak this way. But, like all Americans, he was boiling mad. Finally, in a voice choked with emotion, he said, "I must say that in fifty years of public service I have never seen a note that was crowded with such lies. I never imagined until today that any government in this world was capable of uttering them."

Then he coldly told the two Japanese to leave his office.

In Japan Emperor Hirohito announced to the people,

"We, by the grace of Heaven, Emperor of Japan, seated on the throne of a line for ages eternal, say to you, our loyal

40

Pearl Harbor, December 7, 1941—
"a date which will live in infamy . . ."

and brave subjects: We hereby declare war on the United States of America and the British Empire."

The next day, in America, President Franklin D. Roosevelt read a message to Congress. It opened: "Yesterday, December 7, 1941—a date which will live in infamy— . . ."

With only a single "no" vote, Congress declared war on Japan.

Speaking for a nation united, President Roosevelt said:

"We are now in this war. We are in it all the way. Every single man, woman, and child is a partner in the most tremendous undertaking in our national history."

Three days later, on December 11, 1941, carrying out their "Pact of Steel," Germany and Italy declared war on the United States. Thus, America found herself with *two* wars on her hands.

FRANKLIN DELANO ROOSEVELT: AMERICA'S WAR LEADER

Both Britain and America were fortunate to have great war leaders. Britain had Winston Churchill with his inspiring words and fighting spirit. The United States, too, had a brilliant commander in chief. Together, the two war leaders planned the moves which turned the tide of war in favor of the Allies.

Franklin Delano Roosevelt, 32nd president of the United States, was a tall man with a fine head set on great shoulders and massive chest. In 1921, at the age of thirty-nine, he was stricken with polio. Like many children and adults of that time before the Salk and Sabin vaccines, he was paralyzed from the waist down. He had only partial use of his legs for the rest of his life. That did not stop him. In 1933 he was elected president. It was the same year that Adolf Hitler became Chancellor of Germany.

Roosevelt was a confident man, in full control of himself. He had an electric effect on private and public audiences. He had a good sense of humor and liked to laugh. During the Depression, he inspired his fellow Americans: "The only thing we have to fear is fear itself."

In 1944, in the midst of the war, he was reelected for a fourth term as president—that had never happened before. He led his people to victory, but was not fated to see it.

RISING SUN OF NIPPON

Soon after the sneak attack on Pearl Harbor, Japan began to spread her power all over the Pacific. In a matter of days she attacked Singapore, Manila, Wake Island, and Guam. Japanese troops seemed to be landing everywhere.

Then came a bitter setback for the British. Japanese planes caught the battleship *Prince of Wales* and the battle cruiser *Repulse* without air cover off the east coast of Malaya and sank the two great warships. A weary British garrison surrendered at Singapore. The Japanese also captured the important Burma Road, the supply route from India to China.

It was the same story in the Philippines. Here outnumbered Americans fought heroically, but in vain. General Douglas MacArthur, on orders from Washington, escaped from Bataan to Australia.

"I shall return!" said the general.

At Bataan peninsula the Americans made a last stand. Under command of Lieutenant General Jonathan Wainwright, the Filipino-American defenders tried to hold out. They were

bombarded from the air, pounded with heavy artillery, attacked by infantry units.

The men on Bataan had to surrender. The Japanese took 11,500 prisoners. These unlucky men were sent on a horrible death march. Sick, starved, and miserable, prodded by Japanese bayonets, they were forced to walk many miles to a prison camp. Hundreds perished on the way.

Americans would remember Bataan—just as they remembered Pearl Harbor.

Within four months the Japanese went ahead to overrun the Netherlands East Indies in the south. The Rising Sun of Japan was now dangerously close to Australia and India.

WAR ON THE HOME FRONT

World War II was total war. That meant that civilians as well as soldiers were under attack. There was war not only on the battlefront but also on the home front.

In any major war there are always two fronts—the battle areas where armies fight, and the home front, where the people work hard to support their soldiers. The United States was the only country where civilians were not under attack at home. They were able to put all their energies into production of war supplies.

Within a short time after the Japanese attack on Pearl Harbor, the American people went on a war footing. Millions

Japanese troops
celebrate victory on Bataan.

went into factories and shipyards to make the tools of war and the ships to carry them to the fighting fronts. Workers promised not to go on strike as long as the war lasted. Out of the factories poured planes, landing craft, tanks, trucks, and rifles—all the tools of war.

Americans also started a huge shipbuilding program. Ships were put together in record time for use in the war.

There had been nothing like it in the history of mankind. Americans were enraged by the Japanese attack. They had had enough by now of Adolf Hitler and his wild ideas.

Young people also did their share. They looked in attics, basements, yards, and vacant lots for scrap metal that could be turned into bullets. They found old iron, tin, brass, copper, tinfoil, all kinds of metals which could be melted down and used again. They sold war bonds to help raise money for the costs of war.

These millions of young people were heroes on the home front. They helped win the biggest war in history.

SEESAW WAR IN NORTH AFRICA

By the spring of 1941, Hitler had conquered Europe. Now he could be attacked only from Britain, from Russia, or from

The American war effort produced supply-carrying "Liberty Ships" at an incredible rate. This one, the Joseph N. Teal, was constructed in a total of ten days!

North Africa. North Africa thus became one of the most important battlefronts of World War II.

When the war began, Mussolini sent his troops to North Africa. His strategy was to try to capture the Suez Canal and thus cut off the Allies from the Far East. The British had troops in Egypt, some stationed there before the war and others brought there all the way around Africa. They planned to capture all of North Africa, and then use it as a base for an attack on Hitler's Fortress Europe.

By 1941, Italian troops had already driven 60 miles (96.6 km) into Egypt toward the Suez Canal. Then British forces struck back. Their surprise counterattack carried them halfway across Libya. They captured many Italian prisoners.

Mussolini called on Hitler for help. Together, the Germans and Italians drove the British back into Egypt.

The first round of the Battle of North Africa ended in stalemate.

Round two came in 1942. Once again it was a seesaw battle swinging back and forth. Desert warfare was a story of fast-moving tanks pushing forward through the enemy lines and then retreating across the hot sands.

General Erwin Rommel was the German leader. He was a brilliant master of tank warfare. He was called the Desert Fox because he was as wily and shrewd as a fox. He led his tanks into Egypt.

It was a dark moment for the British. But their Eighth Army, under the command of General Bernard Montgomery, beat the Germans at El Alamein in November of 1942. It was one of the greatest Allied victories of the war.

While Montgomery was chasing the Desert Fox, there came a sensational surprise far to the west in French North Africa. Three Anglo-American landings were made at Casablanca, Oran, and Algiers. Troops, tanks, and tons of supplies

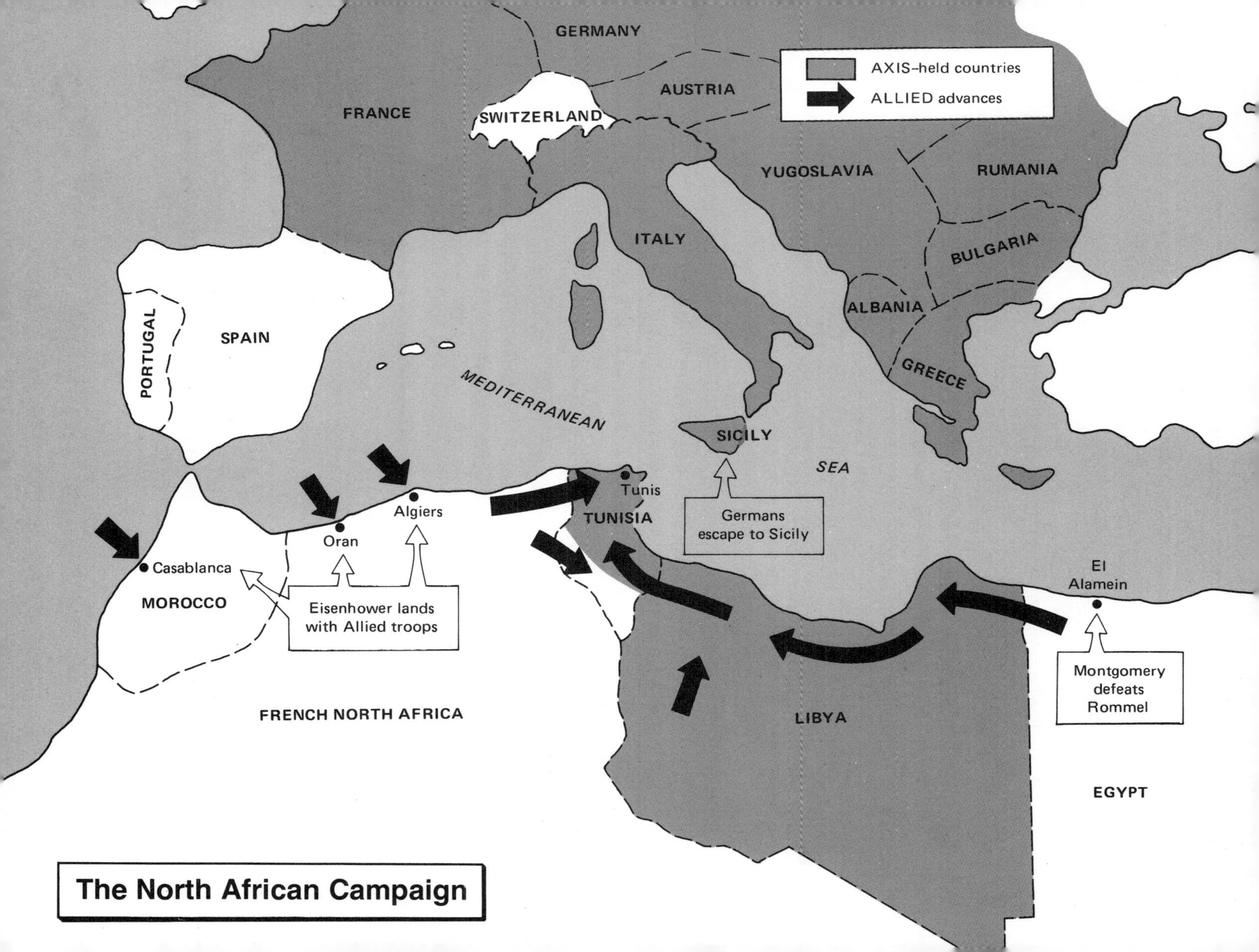
GERMANY
AXIS-held countries
ALLIED advances
FRANCE
SWITZERLAND
AUSTRIA
YUGOSLAVIA
RUMANIA
ITALY
BULGARIA
ALBANIA
PORTUGAL
SPAIN
MEDITERRANEAN
GREECE
SICILY
SEA
Tunis
TUNISIA
Algiers
Oran
Casablanca
MOROCCO
Germans escape to Sicily
Eisenhower lands with Allied troops
El Alamein
Montgomery defeats Rommel
FRENCH NORTH AFRICA
LIBYA
EGYPT

The North African Campaign

were put ashore safely from a vast fleet of ships. It was a magnificent feat. It came as a complete surprise to the Axis war leaders.

The commander of this expedition was General Dwight D. Eisenhower.

The enemy was now caught in a pincers movement from both east and west Africa. Hitler poured thousands of airborne troops into the battle. But it was all in vain.

Round three came in 1943.

Montgomery pursued the Desert Fox westward for more than 1,000 miles (1,609 km). His British tanks moved as much as 40 miles (64 km) a day. And Eisenhower closed in from the west. The Germans were caught in a steel trap.

The Germans fought hard and skillfully. But the end, when it came, came quickly. Cut off by land, sea, and air, without any fuel for their tanks, they were helpless.

What was left of Hitler's African army escaped to Europe. They crossed the Mediterranean between Tunisia and Sicily, the island off the toe of Italy. The Italians lost their African armies and all their colonies on that continent.

Now the way was open to attack Hitler from the south where the enemy was less strongly defended—"the soft underbelly of the Axis," as Churchill called it.

BEGINNING OF THE END

Italy's "Sawdust Caesar" had dreams of empire in North Africa. Those dreams were now blasted. The iron-jawed Mussolini huffed and puffed like a giant frog—until he was on the verge of blowing himself apart.

The Allies had a plan to take care of him. They would

invade Italy from the south and push straight up the peninsula directly to the heart of Nazi Germany.

It began on July 9 and 10, 1943. Powerful Allied armies crossed from North Africa to Sicily, the island which the rest of the big boot of Italy seems to be kicking into the Mediterranean Sea.

By August 17 the Americans and British had completed the conquest of Sicily. President Roosevelt reported happily: "It is the beginning of the end."

In truth, the Italian people were sick of fighting and they had had enough of dictators Mussolini and Hitler.

THE DEAD MAN WHO FOOLED THE NAZIS

Each side used every trick possible to fool the other. The British were skilled in deception tactics to confuse the enemy. In 1943, they put false documents on a corpse to mislead the Germans about an invasion area.

It was called Operation Mincemeat. Just before the Allies invaded Sicily, that soft underbelly of Europe, the British worked out a unique scheme to convince the Germans that the next landings would be in Corsica and Greece.

From a funeral home in central London they got the body of a young man in his early thirties. They gave him the name and papers of a "Major William Martin, 09500, Royal Marines." Into his pockets went false letters that seemed to be from his father, his bank, and his family legal advisor. Bills and ticket stubs went into his pockets, too. He also bore a "code" message: "He might bring sardines with him."

On the evening of April 10, 1943, the corpse of "Major

Martin" was dropped off the coast of Spain by a British submarine. A Spanish fisherman found it and turned it over to the Germans.

Within hours copies of all the papers found on the corpse were sent to Hitler. The *Führer* was sure that the "sardines" meant Sardinia. He sent large numbers of his troops to that island instead of Sicily.

On the night of July 9–10, 1943, the Allies landed in Sicily.

The scheme worked to perfection. It was a clever act which helped to fool the Nazis. Later, a film was made about this "man who never was."

THE ITALIANS GIVE UP

When the Italians saw masses of Allied troops pouring through Sicily, when they saw that all their colonies were lost, they turned against their strutting little dictator with his false promises. In July, Mussolini was arrested by his own people.

After Allied troops had taken all of Sicily, they now crossed over to mainland Italy. On September 9, 1943, the first units landed on the beaches at Salerno. Angered because his

Black troops of the 92nd Division, Fifth Army, start scaling the muddy banks to cross the Arno heading toward German positions.

Italian allies could not stop the enemy, Hitler sent down as many German troops as he could spare to meet the Allies. The Germans fought hard to halt the Allied advance.

British and American troops pushed up the Italian peninsula slowly. It was a costly campaign. By October, however, they had taken Naples. Next came another landing at Anzio.

It took months of bloody fighting, but at last the Allies came within sight of Rome, the city of Caesar and a host of emperors and popes. Rome fell on June 4, 1944. It was the first Axis capital to surrender to the Allies.

From Rome the Allies moved steadily northward through Tuscany, pushing the Germans farther and farther back. At last they reached the Gothic Line, the last of a series of defensive lines that Hitler had set up across Italy.

D-DAY: THE GREAT NORMANDY INVASION

Despite his losses in Africa, Italy, and Russia, Hitler felt sure that he could hold on to his conquests in Europe.

"No power on earth," he boasted, "can drive us out!"

He was talking about what he called Fortress Europe. He had ringed the continent with strong defenses. True, the Allies had broken through his lines on the Italian peninsula, but he was certain about northern Europe. All along the shores of northern France, facing England, he had built a series of strongholds—defended by big guns and tanks.

In Britain, on the other side of the English Channel, the Allies were busy gathering huge masses of troops and supplies. They were going to attack Hitler's mighty defense system and invade Fortress Europe.

54

This was the famous Second Front which the Allies had promised Stalin. (The other front was in the east, where Red troops were smashing the German invaders.)

Preparation for the Second Front was called Operation Overlord. The day of invasion was to be called D-Day.

D-Day was planned to take place in May 1944. But the weather was bad during that month—heavy storms made it hard to cross the choppy Channel. The Allies had to wait for better weather.

General Dwight D. Eisenhower, in command of the giant operation, had to choose exactly the right moment for it to begin.

First came bombing from the air. Great waves of Allied bombers moved on the French coast, destroying roads and bridges. Small commando units—fighters specially trained in sabotage and hand-to-hand combat—were dropped from the air to wreck German radar stations. French resistance fighters, secretly supplied with weapons, turned on the Germans.

Across the Atlantic from the United States poured a stream of war weapons. All England turned into a huge military and supply base for the coming invasion. For months trucks and tanks rumbled along the roads. Planes roared overhead. From artillery ranges came the boom of practice shooting.

Then it came—June 6, 1944—D-Day! It was two days after the surrender of Rome.

At 2 o'clock in the morning British and American paratroopers dropped softly into Normandy. At 3 o'clock heavy aerial bombardment began. At sunrise big guns of the warships boomed. Artificial harbors made of concrete and old ships were towed into place to make the water calm for the invasion. These harbors were known by the code names of Mulberry I and Mulberry II.

At last, from 4,000 transport ships that had crossed the Channel under cover of darkness, a huge army of men began to pour onto the Normandy beaches. The ships shuttled back and forth across the Channel again and again. Warships and a great umbrella of planes protected them. It was the greatest display of military power in the history of the world.

Then suddenly the weather turned rough. Some amphibious tanks, which could be used both on water and on land, ran afoul of the German steel traps anchored along the beaches.

Even so, the Germans were taken completely by surprise. They had made a blunder. Though they expected invasion, they had thought that the weather was not right for it at that time. They canceled a routine boat patrol that might have given them warning.

There was terrible fighting in Normandy on "Omaha" Beach, as the Americans called it. "Utah" Beach, where other landings were made, was taken more easily.

Once the Allies gained a foothold on the beaches of Normandy, they kept going forward. An Allied army of nearly a million men landed in France, followed by a stream of war supplies.

From the south of France, Allied armies began a push northward. This operation was called Anvil-Dragoon. The idea was to catch the Germans in a huge trap.

Hitler was now faced with an Allied *Blitzkrieg* more pow-

*An American tank carrying French
soldiers rolls down the ramp of
an LST (landing ship, tank)
to land on a Normandy beach.*

erful than any he had led in the war. He was being paid back tenfold for the damage he had caused.

The *Führer* and his evil Third Reich were now in serious trouble.

"NUTS!" SAID THE GENERAL

Thousands of stories came out of this war. A famous story of defiance goes like this:

By early December, 1944, American and British armies were ready for an all-out attack on Hitler's Siegfried Line. The Germans, watching closely, decided to make one last desperate attempt to drive them back into the sea, just as they had done at Dunkerque.

The German commander, Marshal von Rundstedt, suddenly attacked in the Ardennes region of Belgium where a single American corps of four divisions held the front. He smashed ahead with one of the strongest tank forces in history. Soon his troops opened a tremendous hole, or bulge, in the Allied lines. This battle, from December 16 to 26, was called the Battle of the Bulge. It was fought almost entirely by American soldiers.

The Americans fought hard. At first, they had no help from the air. The weather was so foggy that their planes could not get off the ground. One American unit was cut off completely at a small place called Bastogne in the middle of the Bulge. It looked like a bad Christmas for the soldiers.

At his headquarters, Brigadier General Anthony C. McAuliffe knew that his troops were greatly outnumbered. An aide came in with a message from the Germans.

"What do they want," asked the General.

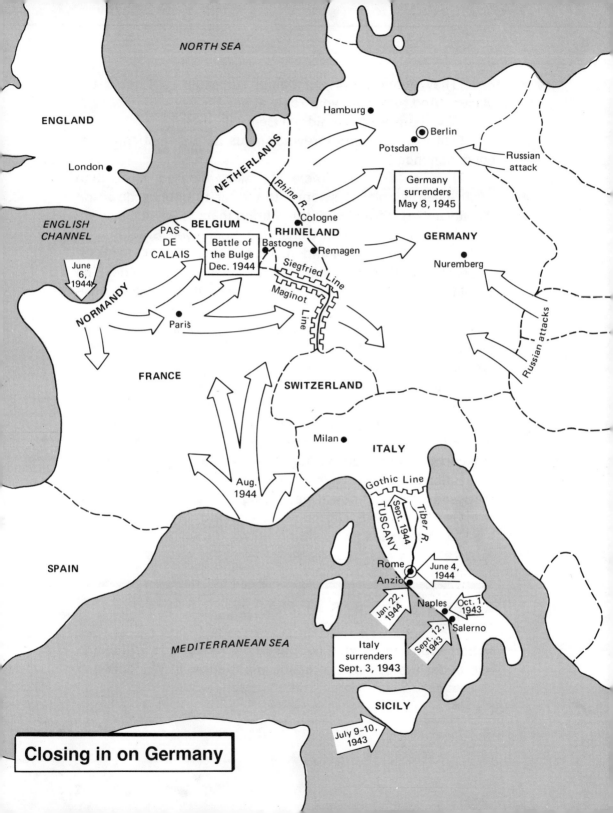

NORTH SEA

ENGLAND

London •

ENGLISH CHANNEL

Hamburg •

⊙ Berlin
Potsdam •

Russian attack

NETHERLANDS

Rhine R.

Germany surrenders May 8, 1945

BELGIUM

Cologne •

RHINELAND

GERMANY

PAS DE CALAIS

Battle of the Bulge Dec. 1944

Bastogne •

Remagen •

Nuremberg •

June 6, 1944

Siegfried Line

Russian attacks

NORMANDY

Maginot Line

Paris •

FRANCE

SWITZERLAND

Aug. 1944

Milan •

ITALY

SPAIN

Gothic Line

Sept. 1944

TUSCANY

Tiber R.

Rome •

June 4, 1944

Anzio •

Jan. 22, 1944

Naples •

Oct. 1, 1943

Salerno •

Sept. 12, 1943

MEDITERRANEAN SEA

Italy surrenders Sept. 3, 1943

SICILY

July 9–10, 1943

Closing in on Germany

"They demand our immediate surrender, sir!" said the officer. "And they want your reply at once."

"Tell them NUTS!" said the General.

That word became forever famous as an American symbol of defiance.

Then, as if by a miracle, the skies cleared. More than 5,000 Allied warplanes swept into the air to pounce down on the advancing German tanks and bring them to a halt.

Meanwhile American Generals Eisenhower, Bradley, and Patton, and General Montgomery of Great Britain sent reserves to Belgium to squeeze both sides of the Bulge. The bewildered Germans were forced back to their original positions.

This was the last German drive of the war. Prime Minister Churchill called the Battle of the Bulge the greatest American battle of the war.

At long last came the invasion of Germany itself.

General Patton's tanks went so fast that they ran out of fuel. By good luck the Americans found a bridge at Remagen across the Rhine. The Germans, making a great blunder, failed to blow up that precious bridge. American tanks sped across it.

Hitler had boasted that his Nazi Reich would last for a thousand years. But now it was facing its end.

On May 7, 1945, Germany surrendered. May 8, known as V-E Day, was hailed as the formal end of the war in Europe.

ALLIES WIN THE WAR AT SEA

In both World Wars what happened on the surface of the seas and under the sea was of major importance. In World War II,

Germany renewed her U-boat campaign with even greater violence. But the Allies were beginning to win this battle of the oceans.

For a long time, Allied scientists worked at top speed to produce devices which could detect U-boats under the sea. They perfected radar, which bounced a signal off an object and made its location known. A special kind of radar, called sonar, was used for this purpose underwater. Once a U-boat was located, destroyers and planes headed for the spot to get the undersea craft.

Keeping U-boats under control was a tough job, because there were 80,000 miles (128,720 km) of seaways, and as many as 3,000 ships had to be protected at one time. But it was done. Ships and aircraft worked together. If one found a U-boat, the other would be called in to help destroy it.

In 1943, the tide of sea battle began to turn against the Germans. It was a critical stage of the war. The U-boat crews were skilled—but their power began to be shattered by Allied sonar. Radar and sonar changed everything—they robbed the Germans of their chief asset—invisibility in the dark.

At the start of 1944 the Germans were losing U-boats at the rate of one a day. Of the 720 U-boats they had sent to sea, at least 640 were sunk. Out of 40,000 men who served on them, 30,000 lost their lives.

It was the same story on the surface of the seas. Allied power struck down one German warship after another.

On December 26, 1943, British warships sighted the German battleship *Scharnhorst,* which was attacking an Allied convoy on the way to Russia with supplies. They sent the great German warship to the bottom of the sea.

The Axis had controlled the seas in 1941. Now the Allies gained mastery.

ISLAND HOPPING
IN THE PACIFIC

Soon after their attack on Pearl Harbor and throughout 1942, the Japanese moved across the Pacific. Before long they had access to huge quantities of rubber, tin, oil, quinine, and other products of the East Indies. They conquered an empire covering a quarter of the earth's surface!

Then the United States Navy began to fight back. Twice, in the middle of 1942, it thrashed the Japanese fleet. Those two victories put a halt to Japanese expansion.

The Battle of the Coral Sea took place in early May 1942. The Japanese and American surface fleets were too far apart to see each other! All the fighting was done by aircraft. American aircraft roared in to smash the Japanese warships. The Japanese had to give up their plan to take New Guinea and move on Australia.

The next month, on June 4, Japanese ships were discovered headed for Midway Island. Again American pilots went into action. They mauled the Japanese ships so badly that what was left of their fleet had to retreat.

The American navy was now on the offensive. It was the

Top: periscope photograph of torpedo hitting, taken from the submarine USS Puffer. *Bottom: depth charge dropped by a Coast Guard cutter explodes during a battle with a Nazi submarine.*

Yanks stop to rest in a deserted Japanese bivouac;
a medical corps officer treats a wounded man.

attacker, instead of the attacked. On August 7, 1942, United States Marines landed on the island of Guadalcanal in the Solomon Islands.

That was the first step in a campaign directed straight at the heart of Japan. The American plan was to move ahead in a series of island "hops." From bases in the Solomon Islands, the Americans would move north to take island after island seized by Japan. Each victory would bring them a step closer to Japan.

First came a hard campaign to capture New Guinea. Then came Tarawa in the Gilbert Islands. Next the Marshall Islands. Then there were the Marianas. As soon as one island was invaded, the Americans were off to the next one. The victories were won at tremendous cost. Thousands of young marines died on these Pacific islands.

By October 1944 the Americans were ready to risk a daring leap to the Philippines. A huge Japanese naval force tried to stop them at Leyte (October 23–27, 1944). The Japanese lost two battleships, four carriers, six heavy cruisers, three light cruisers, and nine destroyers. No navy could recover from such damage. It was a great American victory.

Just as he had promised, General MacArthur returned to the Philippines!

As these battles were going on, there was action also on the mainland of Southeast Asia. Small bands of Allied guerrilla fighters roved behind the Japanese lines causing tremendous damage.

The Allies were getting stronger and stronger, the Japanese weaker and weaker. Slowly but surely the Japanese were forced out of Malaya, Thailand, Burma, and China.

By capturing the island of Okinawa, on April 1, 1945, the Americans moved to within 350 miles (563 km) of the southern tip of the Japanese homeland. U.S. airmen rained tons of bombs on the tinderbox cities of Japan.

The Japanese people were paying dearly for the ambitions of their warlords. They saw at long last that their attack on Pearl Harbor was a colossal mistake.

KAMIKAZES:
JAPAN'S SUICIDE PILOTS

In the closing days of the war, with defeat near, the Japanese turned to suicide as a military weapon. Japanese Premier Kuniaki Koiso issued a solemn warning: "One hundred million countrymen! The enemy now stands at the front gate. It is the gravest moment in our country's history."

The Japanese military decided on a desperate gamble. Their last aircraft pilots were ordered to go into combat with the prospect of certain death.

These suicide planes were called the *Kamikaze* Special Attack Squad. The squad had all the volunteers it needed. The word *"Kamikaze"* means "Divine Wind": in mythology, a typhoon sent out by the sun goddess to wreck an enemy fleet.

Several hundred pounds of TNT were placed in the nose of *Zero* fighter planes. Most of the pilots were youngsters who did not have much training. Before locking themselves in their cockpits to take off on their last journey on earth, they held a formal party. They drank toasts to the emperor, to the life of the Japanese Empire, and to a glorious death. It was a privilege to die for the emperor.

Spaced out for miles off the shores of Okinawa was a huge armada of 1,500 Allied warships, mostly American. They were sitting ducks for the suicide squadrons. Like a swarm of

Allied Victories in the Pacific

angry wasps, the *Kamikazes* descended on the fleet, aiming for the prized carriers.

The pilots came by the hundreds, sacrificing their lives in flaming dives. "Babe Ruth, go to hell!" cried some of them —they thought that to be the supreme insult.

The *Kamikazes* took a heavy toll—34 American ships sunk and 288 damaged. For their "Divine-Wind" vengeance the Japanese paid with the loss of several thousand planes and suicide pilots.

It was a useless gesture. The Japanese Empire was doomed.

SMASHING GERMANY FROM THE AIR

"Not a single Allied plane will appear over Berlin. If it does, you can call me 'Meyer'!"

That's what Hermann Goering said. He was the number two Nazi, head of the *Luftwaffe,* the German Air Force.

A lot of Germans were to call him "Meyer" before long. They were very bitter about it.

In the early part of the war, German planes devastated such great cities as Warsaw, Rotterdam, and London. Then the Allies struck back.

In Frankfurt, Germany, citizens try to clean up the debris that remains more than a year after the war. The man on the right is the mayor.

The first great Allied air attack was on Cologne, a city in the middle of the Rhineland. In the short space of ninety minutes more than a thousand planes showered the city with 2,000 tons of bombs.

In the weeks that followed the Germans were allowed no rest. During the day, American *Flying Fortresses* ranged all over the country. With the accurate Norden bombsight they hit their targets.

At night came the giant British *Lancasters.* Each carried several tons of "blockbusters"—bombs so powerful that one of them could destroy an entire city block.

In between *Fortresses* and *Lancasters* came lighter British planes called *Mosquitoes.* Their buzzing was enough to keep the Germans awake and fearful throughout the night.

By 1943 the Allies had developed a new system of shuttle bombing. Planes would fly over Germany, drop their clusters of bombs, and then head for North Africa. After resting a few days the pilots would return to England by way of Germany, dropping another load of bombs.

One after another the great cities of Germany were reduced to rubble. Hamburg was almost totally destroyed, and other cities were badly damaged. By 1945 Berlin was a shattered ghost city.

It was a sad and terrible business. This was "total" war, invented by the Germans themselves. Civilians as well as soldiers were killed. Factories were destroyed. Homes were smashed.

The Germans were learning the hard way—what you do unto others can be done to you.

Hitler struck back as best he could. His scientists were working on secret weapons which they believed would win the war for Germany. One of these was a flying, or "robot," bomb, called the V-1, or Vengeance Weapon No. 1. It was actually a small pilotless plane carrying a ton of explosives in its nose. Thousands of these bombs were launched from the Continent. They came screaming down on London.

Then the Germans began using the V-2, or flying rocket bomb. Much larger than the V-1, the V-2 could travel at 2,250 miles (3,620 km) an hour. It was silent and gave no warning. It rose over 60 miles (96.5 km) into the stratosphere and came down at terrific speed. It buried itself deeply into the ground before it exploded.

These weapons came much too late. Now Germany was being pounded to pieces by round-the-clock bombings. She could not last much longer.

DEATH COMES TO THREE WAR LEADERS

On April 12, 1945, President Franklin D. Roosevelt died at Warm Springs, Georgia, three months after he had begun his fourth term as President. In his last speech, written to be delivered before Congress, his closing words were, "Let us move forward with strong and active faith."

Roosevelt's death was a sad blow to Americans. Many men, women, and children broke down and cried when they heard the news.

Sixteen days later, death came to the man who had wanted to be Caesar. Benito Mussolini's final boast, while Allied armies poured over Northern Italy, was that he would outdo Hitler in defeat.

"Between the two of us," he said, "the one who dies the more beautiful death will be a greater man in the eyes of history."

*The terrifying robot, a V-1 flying bomb,
caught in searchlights over London.*

There was nothing beautiful about Mussolini's death. He tried to flee Italy in disguise, but he was captured by anti-Fascist partisans.

"Let me save my life," he begged, "and I will give you an empire!"

His captors shot him. They strung up his bullet-ridden corpse by the heels outside a Milan filling station. Angry Italian citizens kicked and spat upon the body of the man who had brought them so much trouble and misery.

Two days later the German dictator, too, was dead.

Hitler was in an underground bunker, or shelter, below the streets of Berlin. Above him was a trembling, shattered city, a flaming ruin. Raving and hysterical, Hitler rushed from room to room. He ordered troops which did not exist into the path of the oncoming Russians.

"The German people are not worthy of me!" he shouted in agony.

Even at the last moment the enraged dictator felt that he would be saved by some miracle. Eva Braun, his wife of a few hours, killed herself. Then Hitler took his own life. The bodies were burned with gasoline in the courtyard over the bunker.

Thus ended the life of one of the most vicious tyrants of all time. It took the combined might of three great world powers to bring Hitler and his lunatic Nazis to the ground.

THE DEADLY A-BOMB

The Japanese were beaten, but they were not yet willing to admit it. By August 1945, their navy and air force were almost destroyed. By their ancient code, however, they were bound to fight to the end.

What could be done to bring these people to their knees? By this time it became clear that the Allies would have to invade the home islands. That would mean that a million or more American troops would be killed or wounded in the last great battle of World War II.

There was another solution.

For years scientists all over the world had known about the idea of nuclear fission—or splitting the atom. If the power of the atom could be controlled, then a bomb of enormous power could be made. Since the start of the war, both German and American physicists had been racing to produce the first atomic bomb. There was real danger that the Germans might win the race.

Albert Einstein, the great German-born scientist, had come to the United States and become an American citizen. He sent a letter to President Roosevelt telling him that such a bomb could be made. At once the president set aside a large sum of money for research.

The scientists got to work around the clock. Among them were the Italian-born Enrico Fermi; Lise Meitner, a brilliant German-born scientist who had escaped from Nazi Germany; the Danish Niels Bohr; the American J. Robert Oppenheimer; and many others. The bomb these scientists produced was a fearsome weapon.

The A-bomb was dropped on Nagasaki on August 9, 1945. It destroyed the city of 250,000 people.

Harry S. Truman, who became president after Roosevelt died, had a hard decision to make. Should he use this terrible weapon or not?

He decided that it was the quickest way to end the war. In the Potsdam Declaration of July 26, 1945, he warned Japan of "dire consequences," and "prompt, immediate destruction," if she did not surrender.

For months a vast American air armada smashed the islands of Japan. Early in the morning of August 6, 1945, a giant Super-fortress named *Enola Gay* took off for Japan. In her bomb bay was the A-bomb—a weapon that had in it the basic power of the universe. The city of Hiroshima, with a population of over 300,000, was to be one of the targets. A small but important Japanese army base was located there.

That one bomb had more power than 20,000 tons of TNT. It had 2,000 times the blast power of the largest bomb ever used until this time. It blew almost all of Hiroshima off the face of the earth.

Houses collapsed like toys. Sheets of flame whipped through the city. Tens of thousands of panic-stricken people fled. Some had their eyebrows burned off. Others had skin hanging from their arms and faces. Terrorized birds flew off in every direction. The hills around the city shook. There was an electric smell in the air. In seconds some 150,000 people were killed or wounded; 75,000 were killed instantly.

Hiroshima was covered with a huge rolling cloud of smoke and dust. First the heavens turned black. Then a giant mushroom cloud floated into the air. Gradually its deadly shape changed into a flowerlike form.

Three days later an even more powerful A-bomb was dropped on Nagasaki, a city of 250,000 people.

THE WAR ENDS

A deep silence fell over the islands of Japan. The stunned and bewildered people could not believe what had hit them. It was enough. Human courage—and the Japanese are a courageous people—could not compete with this atomic monster.

On September 2, 1945, the battleship *Missouri* lay at anchor in Tokyo Bay. Aboard her were the commanders of the Allied forces awaiting the arrival of the beaten Japanese.

Then a little launch appeared alongside the huge ship. The Japanese peace delegates stepped from it and came aboard the battleship. Silently they filed to a table set on the foredeck.

In a clear, firm voice General MacArthur read the terms of surrender. Allied officers present were thinking of Pearl Harbor. MacArthur finished reading and said,

"I now invite the representatives of Japan to sign the instrument of surrender. . . ."

Without a word the Japanese envoys wrote down their names.

"These proceedings are closed," said General MacArthur.

The war in the Pacific was over. It had outlasted the war in Europe by only three months. Proud Japan was beaten.

AFTERMATH

Now the aggressors had to pay for what they had done.

When Italy, Germany, and finally Japan surrendered, the Allies entered the defeated Axis countries. Germany was split into four zones—British, American, French, and Russian. Those nations which had been occupied by the Axis were cleared of enemy troops.

For the first time in her history Japan learned what it meant to be occupied by a foreign people! Her emperor was allowed to keep his throne because he was the only person who could persuade the Japanese people to submit peacefully to their conquerors. The military structure was wiped out. Under General MacArthur, head of the occupation forces, the Japanese began to learn the ways of democracy.

When the Axis prison camps were opened, the world learned in full measure the horrors of Axis rule. The Allies did not let these war crimes against humanity go unpunished. The Nazis responsible for the death of millions of people in gas ovens were put on trial in Nuremberg. Nineteen were found guilty and either executed or sentenced to long prison terms. Hermann Goering killed himself with poison a few minutes before he was to be hanged.

PLANNING A WORLD WITHOUT WAR

After World War II, the United States and the Soviet Union became the two most powerful nations on earth. The great problem now was, how could these two countries live in peace?

Before the war ended, the diplomats of the Big Three— the United States, Great Britain, and Soviet Russia—made temporary plans to insure a peaceful world. At the Yalta Conference, over the period February 4–11, 1945, they had agreed that the liberated, or freed, peoples of Europe should be allowed to form democratic governments of their own choice. But Russia did not live up to her part of the bargain. Before long she set up "satellite" states in Eastern Europe.

The word "satellite" refers to a small star revolving around a larger one. The satellite states were meant to revolve around Russia and do as she told them. Russia seized control of such countries as Hungary and Czechoslovakia in spite of her promises at Yalta.

At the last wartime conference, held at Potsdam, Germany, from July 17 to August 2, 1945, the Allies fixed peace terms for defeated Germany. Then the wartime friendship between the Big Three vanished. Russia turned her back on her allies and tried to draw other countries to her side. Believing she was not safe in a democratic world, she went ahead with a plan to draw more and more countries under Moscow's control.

Americans and British would not accept this state of affairs. The result was a period of Cold War. Nations that had been allies in war were rivals in time of peace.

UNITED NATIONS

After World War I the League of Nations was set up to settle quarrels between nations. It failed, in part, because the American Congress refused membership for the United States.

The United Nations, formed after World War II, had the same goal as the League—a peaceful world. Its charter was

*Churchill, Roosevelt, and Stalin
meet at Yalta in the Soviet Union.*

signed at San Francisco on June 26, 1945, by delegates of fifty countries, including all the Allies.

The UN was to be a town meeting of the world, at which delegates could meet to discuss their problems. The basic idea was that it is better to talk things over than go to war.

The two main organs of the UN are the *Security Council* and the *General Assembly.*

The Security Council now consists of fifteen members, of whom five are permanent (China, France, USSR, the United Kingdom, and the United States). It has primary responsibility for maintaining international peace and security. It investigates disputes between nations. However, it can act only if all the permanent members agree—which seldom happens.

The General Assembly is composed of delegates of all the member nations. (There are now 153.) Each nation sends not more than five delegates. Each country is entitled to one vote. Here, decisions are taken by majority vote. The General Assembly meets in regular annual sessions and in special sessions when necessary. All matters concerning peace may be brought before the General Assembly. The Assembly may call for the use of armed forces to maintain the peace.

Branches of the United Nations work in other ways to prevent war. There are several specialized agencies. The Educational Scientific and Cultural Organization (UNESCO) helps countries exchange useful information. The World Health Organization (WHO) gives advice on public health and control of disease. The International Labor Organization (ILO) helps workers throughout the world. The United Nations Children's Fund (UNICEF) gathers money for poor children everywhere.

The United Nations has had to face many problems, sad to say. The special agencies have done much to promote goodwill and cooperation among nations. But the main organs of the UN have been less successful. Even the best machinery for peace cannot work well if the principal members do not want to cooperate.

It was hoped that the Allies would cooperate after the war. Instead, from its first meeting, the UN has been caught up in an East-West conflict. Instead of promoting peace the UN became an arena for Cold War propaganda battles. The Soviet Union and the United States seldom agree. While the UN performs an excellent service in settling quarrels between minor nations, it does not solve the East-West deadlock.

Yet, despite its faults, the UN keeps the road to peace open. The hopes of mankind still repose in the United Nations.

THE COSTS OF WAR

World War II was the most costly war in history—in loss of lives and property. There are no accurate figures. We do know that millions of lives were lost. Huge amounts of money were spent for war materials and armaments. But how can we measure the cost of broken lives, destroyed homes, the misery and poverty?

Historian Geoffrey Bruun estimates that 10 million men were killed in action in World War II. More than half these casualties were suffered by the Axis states, Germany leading with 3,250,000 battle dead, Japan with 1,500,000, and Italy with 200,000.

In 1946 Stalin claimed that 7 million Soviets lost their lives, but did not specify how many of them in battle. Experts say at least 3 million Russians were battle casualties.

The losses of the western Allies were relatively light: the British lost 400,000 dead, France 167,000, and the United States 325,000.

It is probable that the civilian dead exceeded the total of those killed in battle. It is estimated that there were 34,400,000 injured. Many of these casualties resulted from bombing from the air. In addition, starvation and disease took a heavy toll.

The cost in war materials and armaments and the destruction of property were enormous.

All this was terrible evidence of the meaning of total war.

Some people say that there has always been war and that there always will be. Let us not be too sure of that. Once, men lived by the code of the duel. If a man were insulted, he would demand a fight. That is an old and outworn idea.

So it is with nations. They must learn to settle their problems peacefully.

We live in the age of the atom. Few of us would survive an atomic war. We must live together in one world. We must abide by laws for all peoples—or we will not live at all.

We must win a victory over war itself. That is the hope of civilized people everywhere. As Henry Stimson, U.S. Secretary of War, once said:

The Second World War gave us final proof that war is death. War in the twentieth century has grown steadily more barbarous, more destructive, more debased in all its aspects. The bombs dropped on Hiroshima and Nagasaki ended a war. They also made it wholly clear that we must never have another war.

WORLD WAR II WORDS

A-BOMB: The atomic bomb.

ALLIES: Great Britain, France, United States, Russia, China, and many smaller countries.

ATLANTIC WALL: German control of the ports of Western Europe.

AXIS or AXIS POWERS: Germany, Italy, and Japan.

BANZAI ATTACK: Reckless bayonet charge by Japanese soldiers with yells of *"Banzai!"* This means, "10,000 years, forever!"

BLITZKRIEG, or *BLITZ*: Lightning war: swift-moving air and ground attacks by German armies.

BLOCKBUSTERS: Big British bombs.

BURMA ROAD: Supply route to China.

CASE BARBAROSSA: Hitler's plan for crushing Russia.

COLLABORATORS: Traitors who helped the Axis inside conquered countries.

DER FÜHRER: The leader; used by the Germans in referring to the Nazi leader, Adolf Hitler.

FASCIST: Name of the party founded in Italy by Mussolini.

FFI: French Forces of the Interior: French fighters for freedom from the Nazis.

FLATTOPS: Aircraft carriers.

FLYING FORTRESS: Heavy American bombing plane.

GOTHIC LINE: Final German battle line in North Italy.

GREATER EAST-ASIA CO-PROSPERITY SPHERE: Japanese name for their conquered empire in early years of World War II.

HOLOCAUST: Destruction by fire. In World War II, this refers to Hitler's slaughter of Jews. The victims' bodies were destroyed in huge ovens in German prison camps.

HURRICANE: British fighter plane.

84

IL DUCE: The leader; the Italian Fascists' name for Mussolini.

ISLAND HOPPING: The U.S. plan to hop, skip, and jump from one island to another to the heart of Japan.

KAMIKAZES: Japanese suicide pilots.

LANCASTER: Heavy British bombing plane.

LEND-LEASE ACT: U.S. help for Britain, enacted March 11, 1941.

LUFTWAFFE: The German Air Force.

MAGINOT LINE: French underground line of forts along the Franco-German border.

MAQUIS: French resistance fighters.

MESSERSCHMITT: German fighter plane.

MULBERRY HARBORS: Artificial harbors made especially for the Normandy invasion.

MURMANSK RUN: North Atlantic sea lane for help to Russia.

NAZIS: Followers of Hitler. "Nazi" stands for "*N*ational So*zi*alist".

OPA: Office of Price Administration; U.S. agency to fix wages and prices, January, 1942.

OPERATION OVERLORD: Code name for the Allied invasion of Normandy.

OPERATION SEA LION: Code name for Hitler's plan to invade England. The plan was never carried out.

OPERATION TORCH: Code name for the invasion of North Africa.

PEARL HARBOR: U.S. naval base in Hawaii; attacked by the Japanese on December 7, 1941.

RADAR: The electronic "eye" which sees through fog and darkness.

RAF: Royal Air Force of Great Britain.

RED DEVILS: 1st British Airborne Division.

SECOND FRONT: The Allied line against Germany in Western Europe.

SIEGFRIED LINE: German defense line facing France.

SITZKRIEG: "Sit-down" or "phony" war, on the Western Front, 1939 to early 1940.

SPITFIRE: British fighter plane.

STORMOVIK: Russian ground-strafing plane.

THIRD REICH: Hitler's Nazi state. "Third Reich" means "Third Empire." The first Reich was the Holy Roman Empire, 962–1806; the Second Reich, founded by Bismarck in 1871, lasted until 1918.

TOKYO ROSE: Japanese woman who sent out radio appeals in English for the Allied troops to surrender.

U-BOATS: Submarines.

V-1 and V-2: Vengeance weapons; Nazi flying bombs.

WORLD WAR II DATES

1939 Sept. 1   Germany invades Poland
Sept. 3   Britain and France declare war
Sept. 17   Soviet troops enter eastern Poland
Dec. 17   *Graf Spee* scuttled in Montevideo

1940 Apr. 9   Germany invades Denmark and Norway
May 10   Germany invades the Netherlands, Belgium, and Luxembourg; Churchill takes office
May 26–June 4   Dunkerque evacuation
June 22   French sign armistice at Compiègne
July 10   Beginning of Battle of Britain

1941 Jan. 6   Roosevelt's speech on Four Freedoms
Mar. 11   Lend-Lease Bill signed by Roosevelt
May 27   German battleship *Bismarck* sunk
June 22   Hitler attacks Soviet Union

	Aug. 14	Atlantic Charter signed
	Dec. 7	Japan attacks Pearl Harbor
1942	Apr. 9	U.S. forces on Bataan surrender
	May 4–9	Battle of the Coral Sea
	June 4	Battle of Midway Island
	Aug. 7	U.S. Marines land on Guadalcanal
1943	Jan. 14–24	Casablanca Conference of Allies
	Feb. 2	Germans surrender at Stalingrad
	Mar. 2	Battle of the Bismarck Sea
	July 9–10	Allied invasion of Sicily
1944	June 4	Rome captured by Allies
	June 6	D-Day: Allied invasion of Normandy
	June 13–14	First flying bombs land in England
	June 15	First Superfortress raid on Japan
	Aug. 25	Paris liberated
	Oct. 23–27	Battle of Leyte Gulf
1945	Jan. 17	Russians capture Warsaw
	Feb. 4–11	Yalta Conference
	Mar. 7	Americans cross Rhine at Remagen Bridge
	Apr. 1	U.S. invasion of Okinawa begins
	Apr. 25	U.S. and Russian forces meet at Torgau
	Apr. 28	Mussolini executed by partisans
	Apr. 30	Hitler commits suicide
	May 2	Berlin falls to Russians
	July 17–Aug. 2	Potsdam Conference
	Aug. 6	First atomic bomb dropped on Hiroshima
	Aug. 9	Second atomic bomb dropped on Nagasaki
	Sept. 2	Japanese sign surrender document on U.S.S. *Missouri* in Tokyo Bay

INDEX